FOR MY BOYS

FREE PATTERNS | SEWING TIPS | BLOG | SHOP

WWW.JANETCLARE.CO.UK

ANY QUESTIONS? EMAIL ME: JANET@JANETCLARE.CO.UK

A HEARTY WELCOME...

I found this little Christmas card almost a century after it was sent by 'Eva' in 1915. Isn't it charming? And it got me thinking about the coast at Christmas time, in the very depths of winter when it's bold and bracing. I love the coast then don't you?

So, here's to the coast in winter: to the waves, the spray, the wild salty air and the rosy cheeks...

Hearty good wishes to you!

O GLASSY CALM

'BE CALM AS WATERS
WHEN THE WINDS ARE GONE'

WORDSWORTH

O GLASSY CALM

'o glassy calm' and the other chapter names in the book were inspired by the Douglas Sea Scale which was developed in 1917 to help sailors estimate the roughness of the sea.

It's such an evocative and memorable system that I won't be able to look at the sea without giving it a number again!

In this chapter you will make a very subtle and simple quilt, a hot water bottle cover and there are several boats to draw and stitch too.

There are seas of all sorts, but for the time being all is glassy calm.

BOATS ON THE HORIZON QUILT

The beauty of this gentle quilt is all in its' subtle and toning colours. It is so simple to make that you should be the very image of serene and untroubled calm!

Gather all your fabrics together in a big pile before cutting everything by eye and with scissors. Don't forget you can use the reverse of the fabric too, in fact I probably used the reverse of my fabrics as much as the fronts.

I have chosen to hand tie my quilt- I just knew that attempting to quilt something so freely made would not keep me calm!

Boat

Requirements:

Appliqué: *Grey/brown fabric for boats, Bondaweb*

Free motion stitching: *Stabiliser*

Background: *A wide range of blue, grey and cream fabrics*

Backing fabric and wadding: *60 x 45 inches min*

Binding: *Half yard*

Masts and quilt tying: *Embroidery silks*

Finished quilt measures 60 x 45 inches

Instructions:

1. Prepare fabric: *Cut (with scissors) fabric strips between 4 and 1 inches wide.*

2. Sew background: *Chain-piece all your fabrics together, toning the colours gradually from the darkest to the lightest.*

3. Appliqué 5 boats: *Trace template to create the boats. Arrange carefully on the background. Press in place (see 'How do I?' chapter for tutorial).*

4. Free motion stitching: *Place stabiliser behind the appliqué before free motion stitching (see 'How do I?' chapter for tutorial).*

5. Embroider: *Embroider masts using back stitch. The masts are as tall as the boats are long.*

6. Layer up and quilt: *Tie quilt with embroidery silk.*

7. Make binding: *Cut 3 inch wide strips in different fabrics for double fold continuous binding. Stitch in place, trying to tone the binding in with the quilt.*

O GLASSY
CALM

COASTAL COTTAGES WALL HANGING

Here is a charming row of rather weather beaten cottages, all standing higgledy-piggledy on the shore line. I daydream about living in a little cottage just like them, with nothing at all between me and the sea.

Requirements:

Background: 24 x 11 inches calico
Appliqué: Scraps browns and greys
Quilting: Thin wadding 24 x 11 inches
Wooden frame: 20 ½ x 9 inches

Finished wall hanging measures 20 ½ x 9 inches

Instructions:

1. Prepare fabric: *Cut fabric and wadding to size.*

2. Appliqué cottages: *Trace the cottages onto Bondaweb and press in place (see 'How do I?' chapter for tutorial).*

3. Prepare to quilt: *Trace the feather quilting template using a washable fabric marker or similar. Add wadding.*

4. Free motion stitching: *Add the details on the cottages (see 'How do I?' chapter for tutorial).*

5. Quilt: *Hand quilt in small, even running stitches. Remove fabric markings.*

6. Frame: *Stretch your finished cloth over the frame and staple firmly in place.*

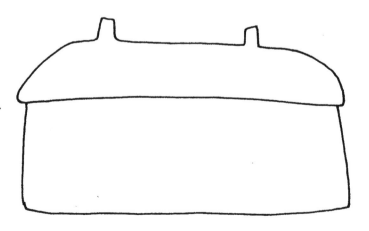

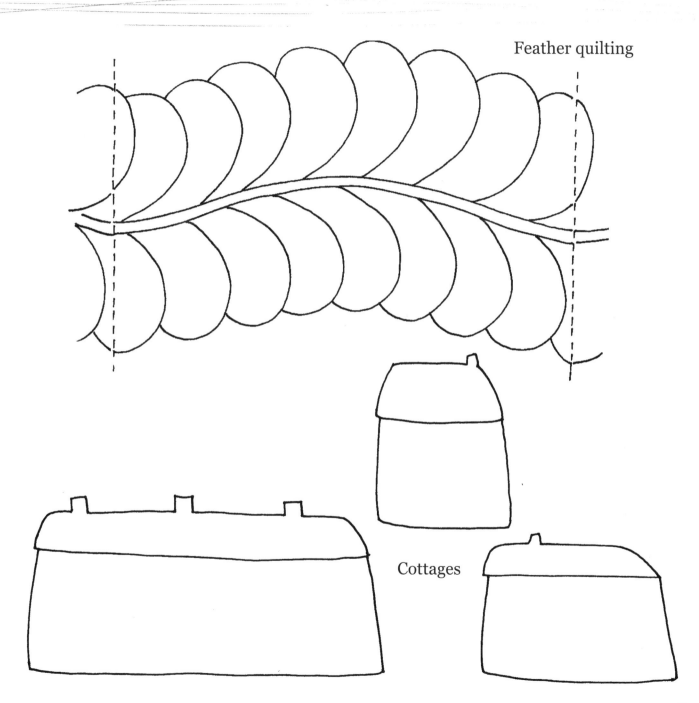

Feather quilting

Cottages

O GLASSY CALM

SHIP HOTTIE

Here is my Henry pretending to be asleep cuddling his new hottie! Made from a piece of wool blanket it's perfect for thawing out little bodies after a bracing day in the fresh air. Although, I've often thought it would be quite nice to have a hottie with me when I'm at the great British seaside!

Instructions:

1. Cut blanket:
   Cut a piece of blanket slightly longer than your hot water bottle and twice the width plus seam allowances.

2. Draw ship:
   Trace the ship onto a removable stabiliser and place on the blanket (or just draw by eye onto blanket).

3. Free motion stitching:
   Stitch the ship (see 'How do I?' chapter for tutorial).

4. Sew:
   With right sides together sew the cover together. Turn and press.

5. Add ribbon:
   Fasten with a bow.

Requirements:

Wool blanket or similar
Hot water bottle
Ribbon
Ship: *Removable stabiliser*

Ship template

SHIP IN A BOTTLE

Well, almost… is a ship on a jam jar close enough? These were great fun to make and have made taking the coffee and sugar on our adventures a little more stylish!

Simply paint the lids of some jam jars with emulsion and draw your ships on the clean jars with a glass pen. I've given you some boat templates to copy, but must apologise to any sailors- I'm sure they're not sea worthy!

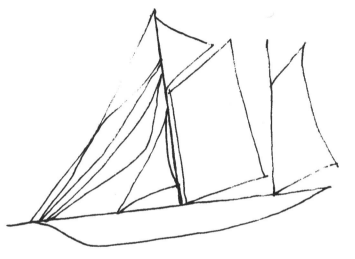

Boat templates

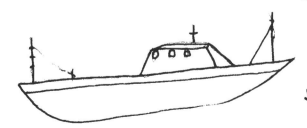

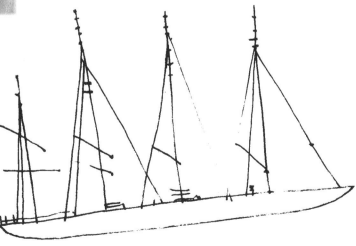

LITTLE IDEAS...

PEBBLES NECKLACES

If you look carefully when strolling on the beach you can find shells and pebbles with holes in them, gather them up and simply thread onto some string.

DRAW AND WRITE ON PEBBLES

Use permanent marker and add to a bowl of beach treasures.

1 RIPPLED CALM

'THERE IS POETRY OF SAILING
AS OLD AS THE WORLD'
ANTOINE DE SAINT-EXUPERY

GOOD OLD BLIGHTY QUILT

I love listening to the shipping forecast when I'm sewing late at night. I take comfort in the fact that we're all safely home when I hear tales of south-westerly gales, storm warnings and moderate seas. Home is rippled calm.

So, here is my quilted shipping forecast. It features hand embroidered names of all the shipping areas and a fair amount of quilting too to add texture to the seas.

It's not a quick project, but we're in no hurry.

Requirements:

36 x 45 inches background fabric *e.g. striped linen*
Fabrics for the pieced land: *20 x 15 inches*
Fabrics for appliqué: *Largest piece 8 x 5 inches*
Fusible web (if using): *1 yard*
Binding: *¼ yard*
Wadding and backing fabric: *36 x 45 inches*
Sewing and quilting threads: *To contrast with your images*
Embroidery threads: *For shipping area names*

Finished quilt measures 36 x 45 inches

Instructions:

1. Prepare: *Cut background fabric to size. Cut fabric for the land into strips between 3 and 4 inches wide.*

2. Sew land: *Chain-piece strips together until you have a random patchwork measuring approximately 20 x 15 inches. Press seams open.*

3. Appliqué: *Trace the large map from separate pattern sheet. Arrange pieces carefully on background. Press. Repeat for the boats, gulls and fish (see 'How do I?' chapter for tutorial).*

4. Prepare embroidery and quilting: *Mark up quilt top with shipping area names, dividing lines and feather wreaths.*

5. Free motion stitching: *Place stabiliser behind the appliqué before free motion stitching the appliqué (see 'How do I?' chapter for tutorial).*

6. Embroider: *Embroider words in back stitch.*

7. Layer up: *Add wadding and backing fabric.*

8. Quilt: *So quick to say, so long to do!*

9. Make binding: *Cut 3 inch wide strips for double fold continuous binding. Stitch in place.*

10. Show your quilt off to everyone – *and never point out your mistakes!*

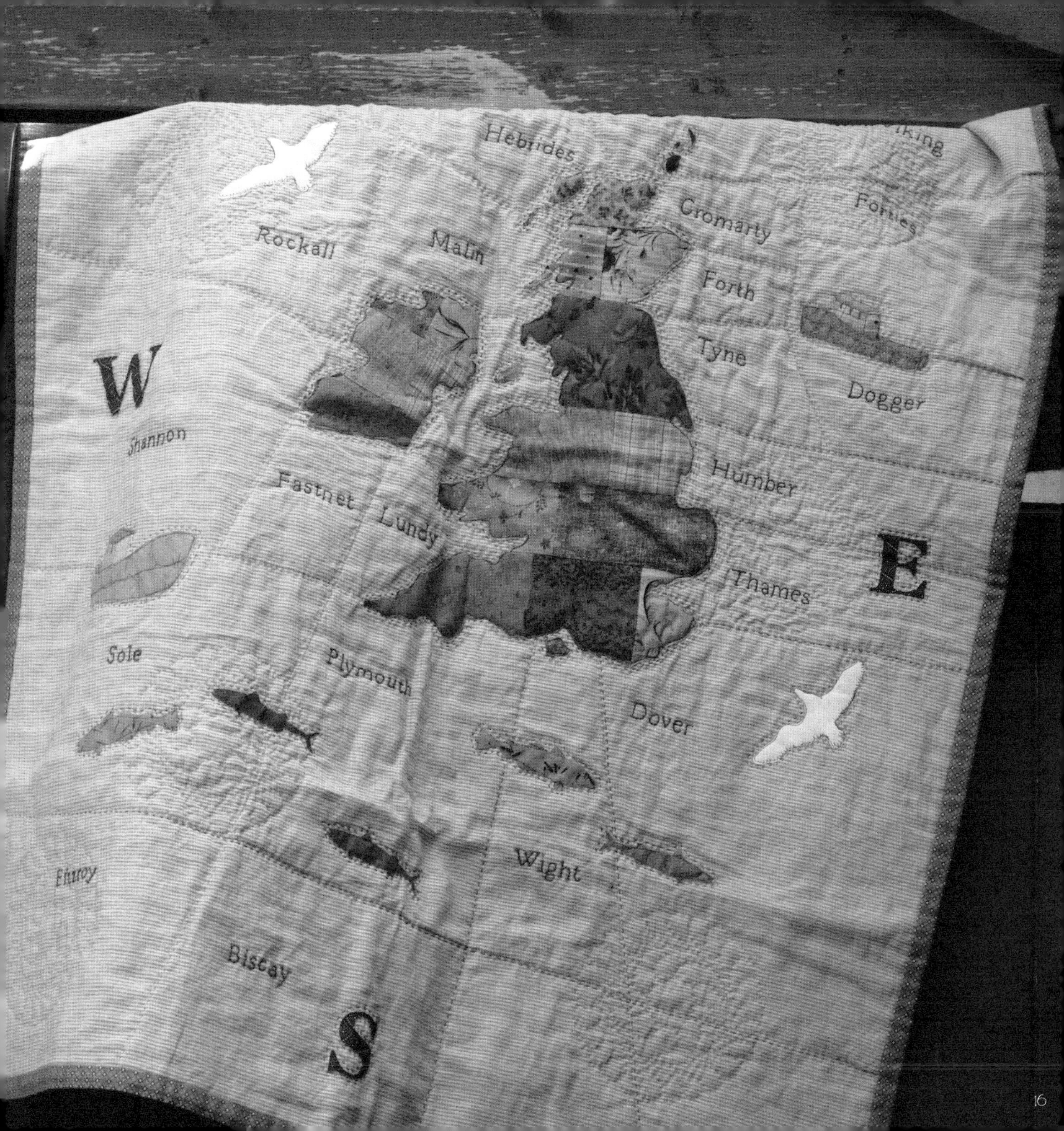

Rockall

Malin

Hebrides

Cromarty

Forties

W

Forth

Tyne

Dogger

Shannon

Fastnet   Lundy

Humber

E

Sole

Plymouth

Thames

Dover

Fitzroy

Wight

S

Biscay

16

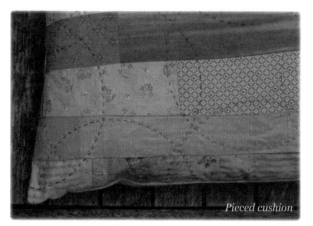

Pieced cushion

CUSHIONS

In my opinion (but sadly not my husband's) you can't have too many cushions. Won't he be pleased to see I've made three more!

Cushions offer a lovely chance to practice new techniques - so be brave, use any of the templates in the book and see what you can create.

Here are some ideas to get you started...

PIECED CUSHION

Take your leftover scraps from making Blighty and sew them together to form a square. Then hand quilt with small overlapping circles.

EMBROIDERED MAP CUSHION

Trace the template and then embroider using back stitch. Add a cross to 'mark the spot' where you live. Hand quilting adds subtle interest.

APPLIQUÉ CUSHION

Choose a few of your favourite templates from the book and simply appliqué to a plain ground. Hand quilt or embroider as desired.

Embroidered map cushion

Appliqué cushion

LITTLE IDEAS

PLATES

Add a quirky touch to plain plates by drawing or writing on them with a porcelain pen (I found mine in the art shop).

BOOK MARK

Here's a thrifty little idea for you! Use up all your leftover pieced scraps to make book marks.

WALL HANGING

A wall hanging I designed for 'Quilt Mania' magazine (issue 84)

SNEW

EW

Fish

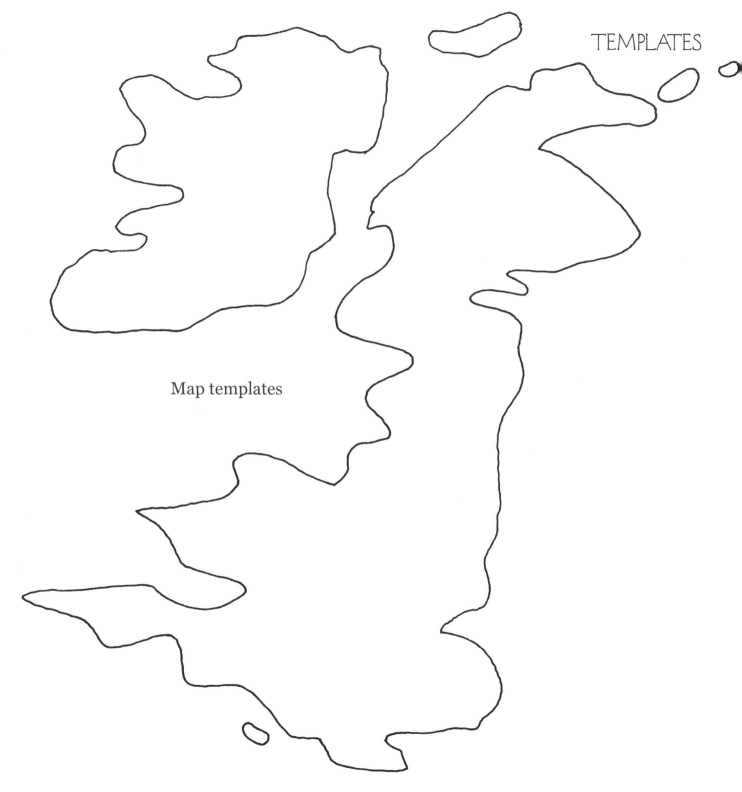

TEMPLATES

Map templates

Bailey   Hebrides

Fair Isle   Viking

Rockall   Malin

Cromarty   Forties

Forth   Sole

Shannon   Fastnet

Lundy

Portland

Plymouth

Fitzroy

Biscay

Wight

Dover

Thames

Humber

Tyne

Dogger

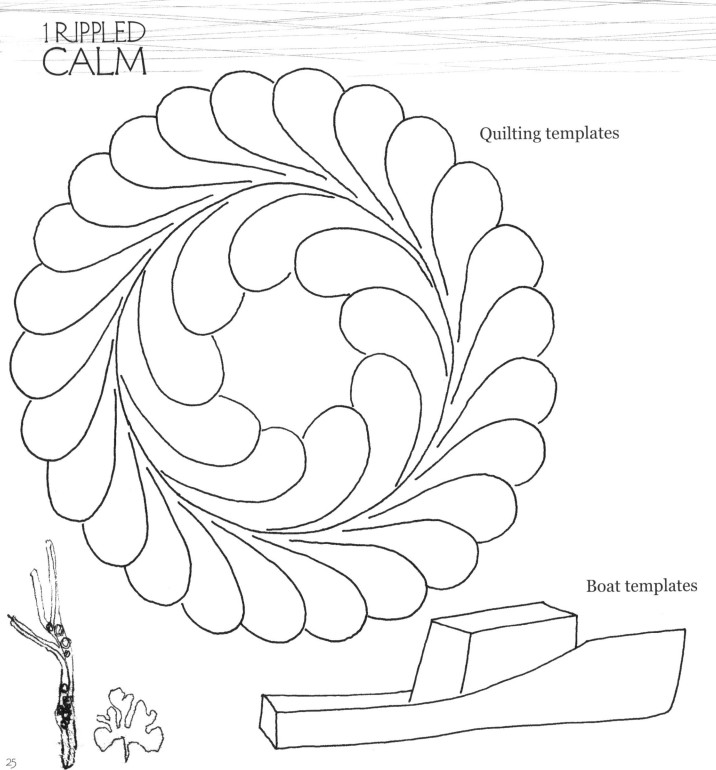

Quilting templates

Boat templates

Gull templates

Shipping forecast areas

BAILEY

VIKING

FAIR ISLE

HEBRIDES

CROMARTY

FORTIES

ROCKALL

MALIN

FORTH

TYNE

DOGGER

SHANNON

HUMBER

FASTNET

THAMES

LUNDY

DOVER

SOLE

PLYMOUTH

PORTLAND

WIGHT

FITZROY

BISCAY

'AND WE FLOAT
AND WE FLY BY'
WILLIAM A. CLARK

2 SMOOTH WAVELETS

2 SMOOTH WAVELETS

For as long as I can remember my parents have lived near the coast and so, to me, home sounds like the Herring gulls calling. I like it.

Apparently, the gull's long call means 'I am here and this is mine' so next time you're at the seaside you'll know what the gulls are saying about your fish and chips! The projects in this chapter are all inspired by picnics at the seaside and the accompanying noisy, hungry Herring gulls.

The seaside just wouldn't be right without them.

SEA GULLS QUILT

This bold and striking quilt was inspired by the busy sky at the seaside. I'm sure someone will tell me that gulls don't fly in formation, but never mind! Arrange your gulls any which way you like and have fun with it!

Requirements:

1 ¼ yd dark blue fabric *(background and binding)*
1 yd wadding and backing fabric
½ yd pale grey or cream fabric for gulls
Sewing threads: *For appliqué*
Knitting yarn: *For hand quilting*

Finished quilt measures 45 x 45 inches

Instructions:

1. Prepare: *Cut background fabric to size, leaving ¼ yd for binding.*

2. Appliqué: *Trace the gulls from separate pattern sheet. Arrange gulls carefully on background. Press (see 'How do I?' chapter for tutorial).*

3. Free motion stitching: *Place stabiliser behind the appliqué before free motion stitching the appliqué (see 'How do I?' chapter for tutorial).*

4. Layer up: *Add wadding and backing fabric.*

5. Quilt: *Using big running stitches hand quilt all over.*

6. Make binding: *Cut 3 in wide strips for double fold continuous binding. Stitch in place.*

7. Show your quilt off to everyone – *and never point out your mistakes!*

TABLE RUNNER

Little gulls this time, swooping and flying on a vintage lace tray cloth.

I dyed this (and lots of other fabric) with a 'jeans blue' washing machine dye giving it a new lease of life and making it much more practical too. Then I chose a subtly patterned fabric for the gulls to add interest.

For your own stylish table runner; simply trace and appliqué the gulls onto your chosen background fabric and stitch round them.

'ALL SHIPSHAPE AND BRISTOL FASHION' TEA TOWEL

This nautical phrase refers to making a ship all neat and tidy- sounds quite a job!

Let's hope you've only got the kitchen to get shipshape!

Trace the words onto your tea towel and embroider with a split stitch.

STICKY GINGER PARKIN

A nice big slice of cake and a warming cup of tea are just
the thing to see you through a blustery day at the seaside.

*This is my favourite cake - it's sticky, spicy and a good
traveller too!*

INGREDIENTS

125g porridge oats
200g caster sugar
1 tsp ground ginger
1 tsp bicarbonate of soda
200ml milk
2 tbsp golden syrup
110g unsalted butter
2 tbsp chopped preserved stem ginger
20cm lined cake tin

METHOD

1. Preheat the oven to 150 degrees C.
   Sift flour into a large bowl and mix
   in the other dry ingredients.

2. Gently bring the milk to the boil
   with the syrup and butter until melted
   then beat into the dry ingredients.

3. Add the chopped stem ginger and
   pour the mixture into the tin.
   Bake for 45 minutes or so.

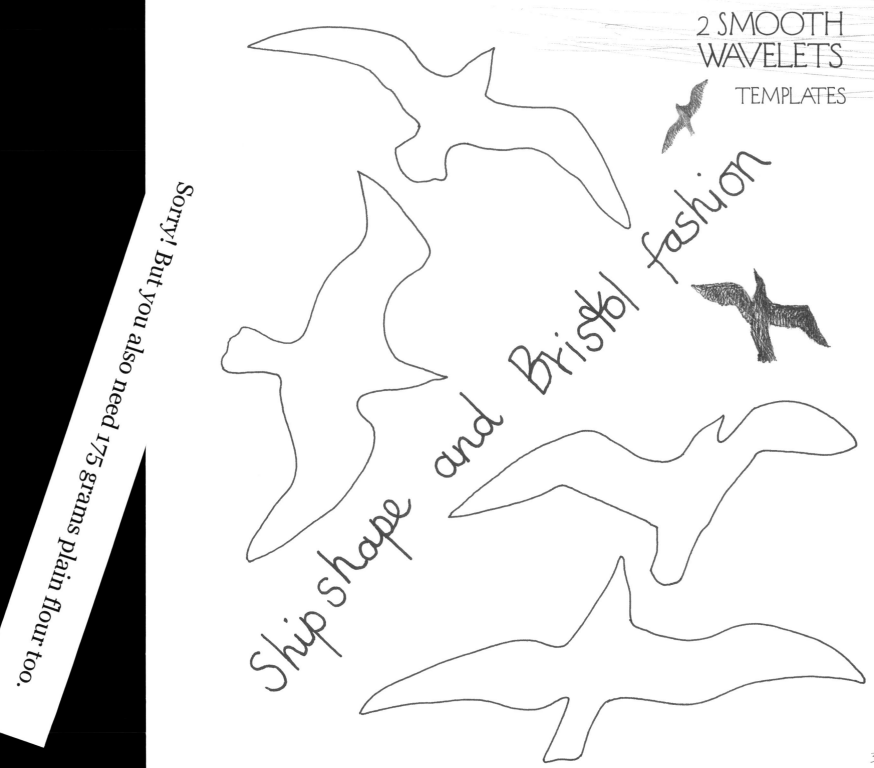

Ship shape and Bristol fashion

Sorry! But you also need 175 grams plain flour too.

LITTLE IDEAS

'SHIVER ME TIMBERS' MUG COSY

Embroider a blanket scrap to keep your tea and hands just that little bit warmer. Fasten with an elastic loop and a button.

NO ORDINARY BIRD

Take inspiration from 'Jonathon Livingston Seagull' by Richard Bach and embroider a napkin or two.

BROOCHES

I've started to customise my denim jacket- adding badges, ribbons, safety pins and embroidered patches anywhere I choose. Look through the book for more little drawings you can embroider.

'LIVE IN THE SUNSHINE,
SWIM THE SEA,
DRINK THE WILD AIR.'
RALPH WALDO EMERSON

3 SCATTERED WHITE HORSES

WHALES QUILT

Now we're a long way from the shore and I'm thinking about the creatures that swim beneath the white horses.

My boys won't leave the Natural History Museum without visiting the blue whale. The largest creature ever born has become something of an old friend. Although, he must shrink in our memory because we are amazed by his size every single time we see him.

We have a soft spot for whales and hope you do too!

Requirements:

19 ½ x 19 ½ inches centre fabric
3 ½ inch wide fabric: *For borders (and binding) approx. 21 yards in total*
Fabrics for the whales: *Largest piece 10 x 5 inches*
Fusible web (if using): *¼ yard*
Wadding and backing fabric: *45 x 45 inches*
Threads: *For sewing and quilting*
Embroidery thread: *For whale names*

Finished quilt measures 44 x 44 inches

Instructions:

1. Prepare: *Cut centre fabric to size. Cut fabric for the borders into 3 ½ inch wide strips of any length.*

2. Prepare border strips: *Chain-piece strips together until you have a long piece measuring approximately 21 yards. Press.*

3. Appliqué: *Trace the whales from separate pattern sheet. Arrange pieces carefully on background. Press in place (see 'How do I?' chapter for tutorial).*

4. Prepare embroidery: *Mark up centre fabric with the whale names.*

5. Embroider: *Embroider names in back stitch.*

6. Free motion stitching: *Place stabiliser behind the appliqué before free motion stitching the appliqué (see 'How do I?' chapter for tutorial).*

7. Sew borders: *Stitch borders to the centre fabric until there are four on each side.*

8. Layer up: *Add wadding and backing fabric.*

9. Quilt: *Machine quilt the borders.*

10. Make binding: *Trim leftover border fabric to 3 inch wide strips to make double fold continuous binding. Stitch in place.*

11. Show your quilt off to everyone – *and never point out your mistakes!*

Physeter Catodon

Orcinus Orca

Balaenoptera Musculus

WIND DOG APPLIQUÉ PICTURE

'Wind dog' is the sailor name for an incomplete rainbow and when one is spotted they know to expect a storm.

My picture shows the calm before the storm.

Requirements:

Background: *12 ¾ x 9 ½ inches pale blue*
Appliqué: *Browns and grey*
Quilting: *Thin wadding 12 ¼ x 9 inches*
Binding: *43 x 3 inch wide darker blue variegated quilting thread*

Finished picture measures 12¼ x 9 inches

Instructions:

1. **Prepare fabric:** *Cut fabric and wadding to size.*
2. **Appliqué:** *Trace the boat and whale onto Bondaweb and press in place (see 'How do I?' chapter for tutorial).*
3. **Prepare to quilt:** *Trace the feather quilting template from 0 Glassy Calm. Draw round plate for the curve of the rainbow. Add wadding.*
4. **Free motion stitching:** *Add the details on the boat and whale (see 'How do I?' chapter for tutorial).*
5. **Quilt:** *Hand quilt in small, even running stitches. Remove fabric markings.*
6. **Make binding:** *Cut 3 inch wide strips to make double fold continuous binding. Stitch in place.*

Sperm whale:

Physeter Catodon

Killer whale:

Orcinus Orca

Blue whale:

Balaenoptera Musculus

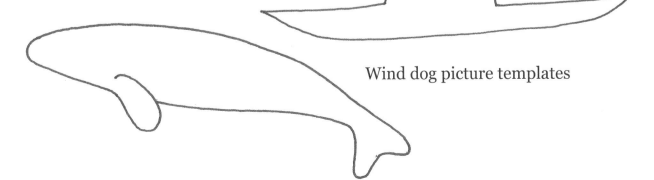

Wind dog picture templates

LITTLE IDEAS

WHALE TOY

This charming whale is simple enough for a child to make. I tie dyed some fabric to use for the whale, which made the project much more fun. You will find the template for the toy whale on the separate pattern sheet.

You could make a whole pod!

DRIFTWOOD WHALE

My Tony whittled this from a piece of driftwood we found on the beach.

WHALE OF A TIME APPLIQUÉ PICTURE

Sorry about the name I just couldn't resist it! This is one of my small patterns. If you can't find an old watch face you can always embroider one.

4 SMALL WAVES

4 SMALL WAVES

When we were little our Irish Uncle Billy took us to the shore (as he called it) and always bought a bag of dried Dulse seaweed. He said it was good for the blood. Unsurprisingly, we didn't like it but we vividly remember those days at the shore with Uncle Billy and his Dulse!

Sailors like seaweed too, because when they spot some drifting about in the ocean they know that land must be drawing near - and a very welcome sight it must be too.

Land ahoy!

QUIET SLEEP BLANKET

The words and inspiration for this pretty blanket are taken from the poem 'Sea Fever' by John Masefield. Quiet sleep and a sweet dream are surely what every weary traveller looks forward to.

Requirements:

Wool blanket or fleece or similar
White fabric for appliqué
Bondaweb
Lace doily
Embroidery silk

Finished quilt measures 35 x 53 inches

Instructions:

1. Prepare fabric: *Press and trim to size.*
2. Appliqué: *Trace the templates. Arrange pieces carefully on background. Press in place (see 'How do I?' chapter for tutorial).*
3. Embroider: *Trace the words onto the lace doily and embroider in split-stitch.*
4. Free motion stitching: *Free motion stitch the appliqué (see 'How do I?' chapter for tutorial) adding masts and ropes to the boat.*
5. Sew lace: *Hand stitch the lace doily in place.*
6. Quilt: *Hand quilt using the circular feather template from 1 Rippled Calm.*

a quiet sleep
and
a sweet dream

44

Seaweed templates

Lettering template

a quiet sleep

and

a sweet dream

Boat template

LAND AHOY!
APPLIQUÉ PICTURE

A little cottage and a lighthouse
welcome a sailing boat safely home.

Requirements:

Finished picture measures 9 x 9 inches

Instructions:

1. Prepare fabric and wadding: *Cut to size.*
2. Appliqué: *Trace the templates. Arrange pieces carefully on background. Press in place (see 'How do I?' chapter for tutorial).*
3. Mark up quilting: *Trace quilting feather template from 0 Glassy Calm.*
4. Add wadding: *Place wadding behind background.*
5. Free motion stitching: *Free motion stitch the appliqué (see 'How do I?' chapter for tutorial).*
6. Quilt: *Hand quilt the feather pattern.*
7. Finish borders: *Turn excess fabric over the wadding and slip- stitch neatly in place.*

Land Ahoy! templates

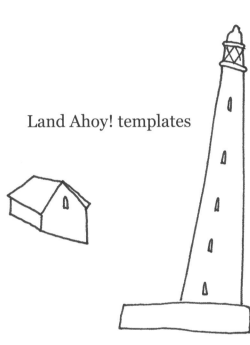

CHEVRON SCARF

This will keep you warm on a breezy day at the apricot and peach (that's beach in cockney rhyming slang).

You will have plenty of yarn leftover, but I couldn't resist using all those charming colours.

Requirements:

4mm (size 8) needles

1 x ball 'Freedom Sincere D.K 100% organic cotton' in these six colours:

Cream 601	*Hessian 602*
Ammonite 603	*Slate 607*
Ocean 608	*Glacier 609*

Instructions:

Cast on 30 stitches.

1st row (wrong side): *Purl*

2nd row: *Knit 1, increase in next stitch by knitting into the front and back, knit 4, slip 1, knit 1, pass slip stitch over, knit 2 together, knit 4 * increase in each of next 2 stitches, knit 4, slip 1, knit 1, pass slip stitch over, knit 2 together, knit 4 repeat from * to last 2 stitches, increase in next stitch, knit 1.*

3rd row: *Purl*

4th row: *Repeat 2nd row.*

Change colour. *Repeat these 4 rows in each colour until scarf is the desired length.*

HOLD FAST BAG

Sailors often had 'hold fast' tattooed across their knuckles to guard against falling when they went aloft.

As falling off rigging isn't that likely in my line of work I've settled for stitching 'hold fast' onto this generously sized bag! Pack it full of life's essentials - *and don't forget your knitting!*

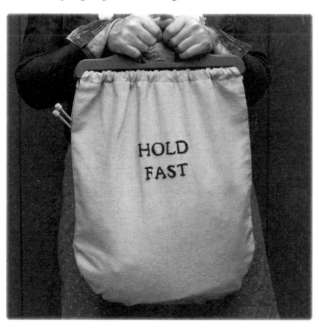

Requirements:

> 1 pair bag handles: *12 ½ inches long*
> Paint
> Linen: *½ yard*
> Lining: *½ yard*
> Embroidery silk

Finished bag measures 15 x 18½ inches

Instructions:

1. Paint handles: *Lightly sand handles and paint.*
2. Prepare fabric: *Cut two 15 ½ x 20 inch pieces linen and two the same for linings. Draw round a plate to make curved corners.*
3. Embroider: *Trace 'hold fast'. Embroider in split stitch.*
4. Attach lining to front and back: *With right sides together sew lining to the front and back of the bag, leaving an opening at the top of each for turning. Clip curves. Turn right side out and press. Sew openings closed.*
5. Sew bag: *Hand sew front and back of the bag together at sides stopping 6 inches away from top to allow for easier access.*
6. Attach handles: *Insert fabric into handles, and stitch down firmly.*

HOLD FAST

LITTLE IDEAS

SEAWEED EMBROIDERY

Look... seaweed can be just as pretty as flowers!

HANKIES

Embroider fabric squares with your favourite phrase before rolling the hems.

LACE BRACELET

Dye some lace to make a light and pretty bracelet.

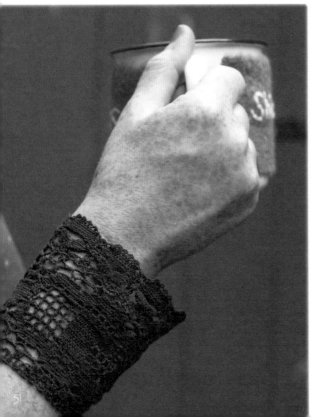

5 MANY WHITE CAPS

'HEAVED AND HEAVED,
STILL UNRESTINGLY HEAVED
THE BLACK SEA'
MOBY DICK

5 MANY WHITE CAPS

The sea is mighty rough now and there are many white capped waves. But the harbour is in sight, and we are nearly home.

Next time 'yours' travel send them off into the world with homemade messages to watch over them and bring them safely home to you: journey's end.

I MUST GET BACK TO THE SEA QUILT

Isak Dinesen said that the cure for anything was saltwater- sweat, tears or the sea.
I heartily agree, but of the three I'll choose the sea every time.

So, this is the cure for anything in quilt form.

Requirements:

Pale fabrics for centre: *10 ½ inch squares*
Pale fabrics for borders: *3 x 15 ½ inches max*
Fabrics for appliqué
Fusible web (if using): *1 yard*
Binding: *¼ yard*
Wadding and backing fabric: *45 x 45 inches*
Sewing and quilting threads to contrast with your images

Finished quilt measures 45 x 45 inches

Instructions:

1. Prepare: *Cut nine 10 ½ inch squares and strips 3 x 15 ½ inches long (maximum) for borders.*

2. Appliqué: *Using templates throughout the book appliqué each square. Arrange pieces carefully on background. Press. See 'How do I?' chapter for tutorial.*

3. Free motion stitching: *Place stabiliser behind the appliqué before free motion stitching the appliqué (see 'How do I?' chapter for tutorial).*

4. Add borders: *Sew borders to each side of central squares. Trim to size.*

5. Piece top: *Sew blocks together into three rows of three.*

6. Layer up: *Add wadding and backing fabric.*

7. Quilt: *Machine quilt round the blocks.*

8. Make binding: *Cut 3 inch wide strips for double fold continuous binding. Stitch in place.*

9. Show your quilt off to everyone – *and never point out your mistakes!*

KISS ME QUICK PICTURE

Do you remember donkey rides and 'kiss me quick' hats at the seaside? *Those were the days!*

Requirements:

Box frame: *11½ x 7½ inches*
Paint
Alphabet tiles or similar
Toy donkey (optional)
Background Fabric: *12 x 8 inches*
Fabric scraps for appliqué

Instructions:

1. Paint: *Remove glass from box frame and paint.*

2. Prepare fabric: *Cut wadding and background fabric to size.*

3. Appliqué: *Trace the templates. Arrange pieces carefully on background. Press in place (see 'How do I?' chapter for tutorial).*

4. Free motion stitching: *Free motion stitch the appliqué (see 'How do I?' chapter for tutorial) adding numbers to the beach huts and a line to the kite.*

5. Quilt: *Hand quilt using the feather template from 0 Glassy Calm.*

6. Frame: *Glue appliqué picture in place. Replace glass.*

7. Decorate frame: *Attach 'kiss me quick' in alphabet tiles or similar to the top of the box frame and add a toy donkey if you wish.*

ANTI-DROWNING SOCKS

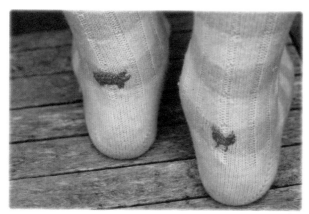

I read somewhere that sailors used to tattoo a chicken on one ankle and a pig on the other to prevent drowning.

I really have no idea if this is true or how it could possibly have been thought to work, but I couldn't resist making some anti-drowning socks anyway.

Be sure to make a pair for every swimmer and sailor in your family!

Anti-drowning socks templates

Kiss me quick picture template

LITTLE IDEAS

WISH YOU WERE HERE BLANKET

Write in a large, flowing hand and embroider onto the border of a throw.

MESSAGES IN BOTTLES

Now, I couldn't write a coastal book and not throw a message in a bottle into the sea could I! It was great fun, but I still daydream about discovering a real one.

LUGGAGE TAG

If they must leave you can at least send them off with a little piece of home.

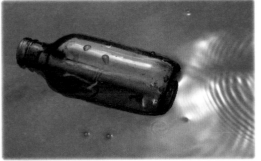

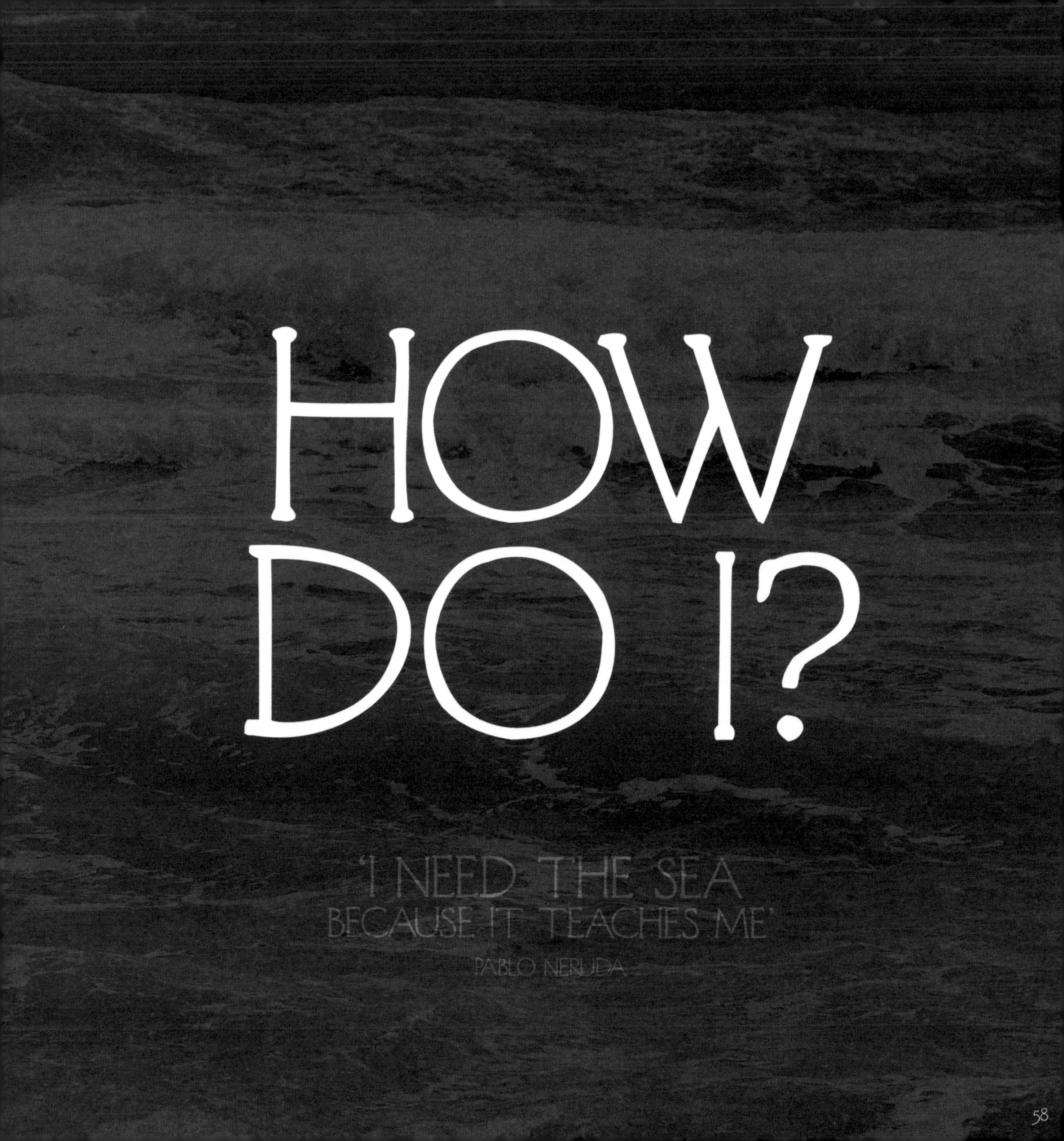

HOW DO I?

'I NEED THE SEA
BECAUSE IT TEACHES ME'
PABLO NERUDA

HOW DO I?

I hope you are inspired to get stitching now that you have looked through my book! I'd love you to create your own designs so, please adapt the patterns as you wish...

...go on, make them your own!

I love to draw with my sewing machine - and have used fusible web (Bondaweb) appliqué and free motion stitching for all the projects in the book.

Templates for almost any technique are simply line drawings, so satin stitch, needle turn or button hole your appliqué - it's your choice. Just remember that you may need to add seam allowance depending on the method you choose.

As you will have seen the instructions in the book are not much more than the order in which to do things, which is all you need if you have some experience. However, if you are a beginner there are plenty of excellent tutorials on 'You Tube' or contact your nearest quilt shop and ask about workshops. You could always come on one of mine!

So, I have concentrated here on giving good clear instructions for my fusible appliqué and free motion stitching technique.

This is how I do it...

FABRIC
Rummaging through your stash and choosing fabrics is one of the little pleasures in life isn't it? Somehow, I seem to have a never ending supply of scraps and as I like to use up what I already have, most of my quilts are scrap quilts. I often use the reverse of a printed fabric as the right side as it gives a lovely faded quality. I'll use any fabric I like, be it patchwork, dressmaking or recycled clothing. I don't worry if it's not 100% cotton.

THREADS
I use a polyester thread because I find it snaps and frays less easily. I generally use just three colours: one the colour of dust, a dark grey and a brown. I personally, think black thread looks too heavy.

WADDING (BATTING)
I generally use *'Hobbs Heirloom Premium Cotton Blend 80/20'*.

FUSIBLE WEB
I use *'Bondaweb'*. Other products are available but I always use this one because I like it.

EMBROIDERED

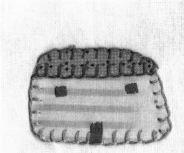

NEEDLE TURN APPLIQUÉ

FUSIBLE APPLIQUÉ & HAND STITCHED BUTTONHOLE

FUSIBLE APPLIQUÉ & MACHINE STITCHED BUTTONHOLE

HOW DO I... APPLIQUÉ

Requirements:

Bondaweb: *Or similar fusible web*
Paper scissors and small sharp fabric scissors
Pencil
Templates
Iron and board
Fabrics
Sewing machine thread
Embroidery silk

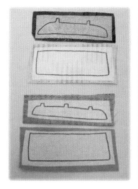

1. TRACE TEMPLATES ONTO FUSIBLE WEB

You may find it easier to photocopy the templates in this book, but please do this only for your own personal use. If you want you can make them bigger or smaller too.

The templates are reversed in the book, so when they are traced and ironed onto the fabric they are facing the correct way.

The following instructions are specifically for 'Bondaweb', so please check the application instructions for your fusible web brand.

 Lay a piece of Bondaweb (paper side up) over the template and trace with a sharp pencil or pen.

2. IRON TEMPLATES ONTO FABRIC

Cut the traced templates out with paper scissors leaving a small seam allowance all round. Place the templates paper side up on the reverse of your chosen fabrics.

Iron to fix in place and then cut them out as carefully as you can on your traced pencil lines.

3. POSITION APPLIQUÉ

Peel off the backing paper, if this is tricky, scratch the middle with a pin. Position all the pieces in exactly the right place (place roofs on top of the building) before finally ironing them down on the background fabric. Be careful because they can't be moved without leaving a sticky residue on the fabric.

4. SET UP YOUR SEWING MACHINE

For most machines this means:

⚓ Lowering the feed dogs/ teeth

⚓ Choosing the darning foot (circular or horseshoe shaped, with a spring)

My machine is happier free motion stitching if it has a new needle - *did you know you're supposed to change your needle after five hours of sewing time?*

I also select the needle down position, so that when I take my foot off the pedal the needle stays in the fabric and I can have a little rest without losing my place.

5. FREE MOTION STITCHING

I've said in the pattern instructions to add a stabiliser or similar behind the areas to be free motion stitched to help prevent the fabric puckering. However, I don't always do this- so see what thickness of fabric your machine is happy to stitch through nicely, you may not need it either.

Now, there's nothing else for it, you just have to start. It may end up in the bin, you may get a bobbin-y mess or a broken needle, but what does it matter?

Remember that you (and not the machine) must move the fabric and control the length of the stitches. If you were drawing with a pencil and paper, you'd move the pencil, but here you move the paper.

HOW DO I... APPLIQUÉ

THINGS TO BEAR IN MIND...

⚓ Look where you are going - not where you've been, it's too late for that!

⚓ Don't press the fabric down - it's not going anywhere, just guide it with your finger tips.

⚓ Don't swivel the fabric round as you might if you were zigzagging round an appliqué, keep the fabric facing the same way at all times.

⚓ Try not to put your foot to the floor! A nice steady flowing speed is what you want.

⚓ If you are getting hundreds of tiny stitches you are going too fast and moving the fabric too slowly.

⚓ If you are getting enormous stitches you are going too slow and moving the fabric too fast. It really doesn't matter if all your stitches are the same length (mine certainly aren't) but the overall effect should be even.

⚓ Remember that the Bondaweb has secured the appliqué to the background fabric, so your stitches are purely decorative.

⚓ Life is too short to un-pick free motion stitching. So if you can, just throw your mistakes in the bin.

Now, be nice to yourself and have an honest look at my stitches - they're not all perfect either are they?

Forth

Tyne

Humber

HOW DO I... EMBROIDERY

TRACING TEMPLATES ONTO FABRIC

I use a water soluble pen to mark up embroidery or quilting patterns onto fabric. If the fabric is hard to see through when tracing hold the template and the fabric up to a window and trace them that way.

I have written instructions for my favourite stitches...

BACK STITCH

This is a very useful stitch as it forms a nice solid outline, making it perfect for embroidering words and shapes.

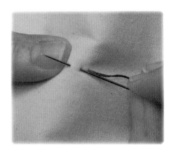

1. Thread the needle with 3 strands of embroidery silk. Knot one end. Come through the fabric so the knot is on the back. Stitch from right to left.

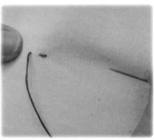

2. Take one stitch bringing the needle back up another stitch length away. Pull thread through so it rests on the fabric.

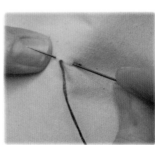

3. Then go backwards to meet the previous stitch, bringing the needle back up another stitch away. Continue in this way.

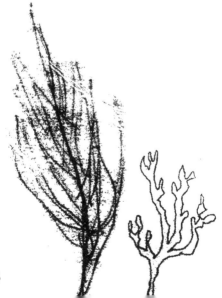

FRENCH KNOTS

These are my favourite embroidery stitches!
French Knots are literally knots which sit on top of the fabric.

1. Start in the same way as for back stitch (A).

2. Hold the embroidery thread in your left hand about an inch away from the fabric. Hold the needle horizontally to the thread.

5. Guide the thread through the fabric so it lays neatly.

3. Wrap the thread twice around your needle from front to back.

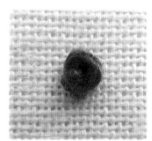

5. *Finished!*

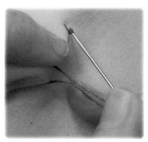

4. Keeping the thread securely wrapped round the needle, push the needle down through the fabric, slightly above A.

AND FINALLY,
PLEASE BE
PROUD
OF YOUR
QUILTS...

...SHOW THEM OFF TO EVERYONE
AND STOP POINTING OUT YOUR MISTAKES!

INDEX

Here's my little guide to help you find the right page...

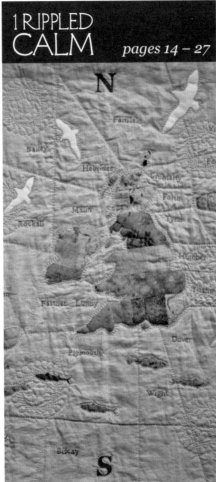

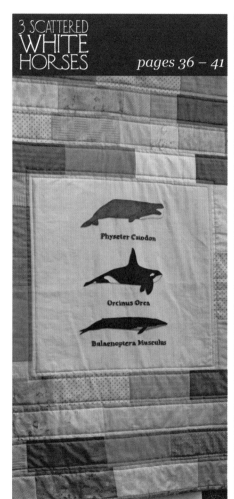

3 SCATTERED WHITE HORSES

Physeter Catodon

Orcinus Orca

Balaenoptera Musculus

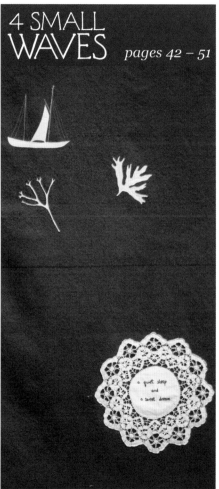

4 SMALL WAVES

a quiet sleep
and
a sweet dream

5 MANY WHITE CAPS

HOW DO I?